Practical Apache Lucene 8

Uncover the Search Capabilities of Your Application

Atri Sharma

Apress®

Practical Apache Lucene 8

Atri Sharma
Bengaluru, Karnataka, India

ISBN-13 (pbk): 978-1-4842-6344-0   ISBN-13 (electronic): 978-1-4842-6345-7
https://doi.org/10.1007/978-1-4842-6345-7

Managing Director, Apress Media LLC: Welmoed Spahr
Acquisitions Editor: Celestin Suresh John
Development Editor: Matthew Moodie
Coordinating Editor: Divya Modi

Cover designed by eStudioCalamar

Cover image designed by Pixabay

Distributed to the book trade worldwide by Springer Science+Business Media New York, 233 Spring Street, 6th Floor, New York, NY 10013. Phone 1-800-SPRINGER, fax (201) 348-4505, e-mail orders-ny@springer-sbm.com, or visit www.springeronline.com. Apress Media, LLC is a California LLC and the sole member (owner) is Springer Science + Business Media Finance Inc (SSBM Finance Inc). SSBM Finance Inc is a **Delaware** corporation.

For information on translations, please e-mail booktranslations@springernature.com; for reprint, paperback, or audio rights, please e-mail bookpermissions@springernature.com.

Apress titles may be purchased in bulk for academic, corporate, or promotional use. eBook versions and licenses are also available for most titles. For more information, reference our Print and eBook Bulk Sales web page at www.apress.com/bulk-sales.

Any source code or other supplementary material referenced by the author in this book is available to readers on GitHub via the book's product page, located at www.apress.com/978-1-4842-6344-0. For more detailed information, please visit www.apress.com/source-code.

Printed on acid-free paper

Dedicated to my mentors (Merlin Moncure, Mike McCandless, and Adrien Grand).

Dedicated to my family.

Dedicated to the Almighty.

Table of Contents

TABLE OF CONTENTS

About the Author

 **Atri Sharma** is a distributed systems engineer with a background in database kernel engineering and search. He has worked extensively on the kernel of many relational and nonrelational database engines(PostgreSQL, Greenplum, HAWQ, RethinkDB) and is currently working on scaling search to the next level.

He is an Apache Lucene/Solr Project Management Committee (PMC) member and is noted for building features like scalable multithreaded searching, circuit breakers, and rate limiters.

About the Technical Reviewer

 **Subhasis** has more than 17 years of industry experience in developing high performance enterprise products, of late with a focus on big data, data engineering, data analytics, and data science areas using Python, Apache Spark (PySpark), Azure Databricks, and related big data tech stack. Throughout his career, he has contributed in several professional function areas like development, QA, technical product owner, architect, and management. He started experimenting with Apache Lucene at an early stage of its release. He has significant experience in the ELK (Elasticsearch, Logstash, Kibana) stack as well.

Acknowledgments

I would like to acknowledge the Lucene/Solr community for the great product that they have built and the support they provided me when I was writing this book.

Introduction

Lucene has singlehandedly conquered the world of search. This project has come a long way in the context of features and user base from its initial days when being developed by Doug Cutting.

Fast forward, and the world is changing. With the advent of big data and machine learning, Lucene has to embrace the upcoming change and ensure that the search quality that people have come to expect of the project remains constant.

Lucene 8 is a step in that direction. With major new features introduced into the system, users need an updated look at how to use Lucene, which this book provides.

CHAPTER 1

Hola, Lucene!

Welcome to your journey into the mystic and fun world of search!

This chapter discusses information-retrieval (IR) systems, focusing on Lucene, and includes a number of terms and key bits of information that you will find handy as we delve deeper into the innards of Lucene and build some cool applications.

Before we begin, let's review some commonly asked questions and their answers.

Is Lucene a search engine?
I would generally respond, "Well, yes and no."

Lucene is a library and platform used to build a variety of IR systems, search engines being the most well known. Other areas where Lucene applies include the following:

- *Document analytics*: Loading and traversing text documents based on some given criteria, finding the top terms from documents, aggregating on specific fields.

- *Log analytics*: Analyzing application logs with high-performance dashboards built directly on top of Lucene.

- *Geospatial search*: With the recent advent of geospatial queries and data structures, Lucene is fast becoming a popular choice for indexing latitudinal and longitudinal data and queries such as colocation searches.

© Atri Sharma 2020
A. Sharma, *Practical Apache Lucene 8*, https://doi.org/10.1007/978-1-4842-6345-7_1

Do I need a background in information retrieval?

A background in IR is good to have, but it is not mandatory in your quest to understand Lucene. Although this book covers some background theory, any complex information is explained in such a way as to allow you to build a contextual understanding.

Note   Information retrieval is a vast subject, and this book does not aim to be exhaustively authoritative on the topic. Instead, this book focuses on enhancing your understanding of Lucene. For a more robust understanding of IR in general, consult an IR book to complement this one. Introduction to Information Retrieval by Manning is a good reference book to start with.

Does Lucene support SQL or SQL dialects?

No, Lucene has a set of supported queries (discussed in further chapters). You can use those queries, however, to construct execution plans that can be derived from SQL-ish languages. Some engines have done exactly that, but Lucene has no native support for it.

Lucene is a library that enables you to build your search application. Use Lucene when you need fast indexing and search capabilities in your application. Lucene puts a lot of power in the user's hands, but with great power comes great responsibility. So, it is crucial that the discerning user understand trade-offs and the best-fit cases for Lucene's more advanced features (as discussed in later chapters).

Key Features of Lucene

Lucene has been around for a while, and a number of its features and capabilities have made it quite popular, including the following:

- *Scalable, high-performance indexing*: Lucene enables very fast indexing (over 150GB/hour on modern hardware).

- *Incremental indexing*: Indexes are added as new documents come in, with no need to modify existing indexes (and thus avoiding excess index churn).

- *Top N queries*: Lucene is efficient at scanning through large volumes of data and getting the top N documents which match the query, ranked by the scoring function used.

- *Myriad query types*: Phrase queries, wildcard queries, proximity queries, range queries, and more.

- *Single-field and multifield searching*: Lucene allows searching on a single field or multiple fields — allowing ranking across multiple fields.

- *Sorting and faceting*: Lucene allows ordering results on a specific field (think of SQL ORDER BY). Lucene also allows faceting on different attributes (think of SQL GROUP BY).

- *Multi-index searches*: Lucene allows a single query to query multiple indices and then merge results from all of the indices to a final result set.

- *Concurrent indexing and searching*: Lucene allows using multiple threads for a single indexing or a search request. This can speed up the performance of a single request significantly.

- *Highlighting, joins, and result grouping*: Lucene allows joins across different indices with certain conditions.

- *Pluggable ranking models*: Including the vector space model and Okapi BM25.

- *Custom codecs for storage*: It is possible to implement and use custom storage formats in Lucene, thus allowing flexibility when using Lucene in the search application.

Although by no means comprehensive, the preceding list highlights some of the more popular features available in Lucene that enable you to build high-performance systems while maintaining a high degree of relevance in the returned results.

Information Retrieval Basics

Before delving deeper into the innards of Lucene, let's review what search in IR systems is really about. Although this discussion does not go into the full complexity of IR, it should allow you to grasp the finer details of Lucene as we progress.

Search, in the context of IR systems, is the art of extracting information with high relevance for a given query.

Indexing, in the context of IR systems, is building inverted indexes from the given text. The process is described in the chapter on indexing. Note that the indexing referred to here and in later chapters differs from typical indexing in relational database systems. Relational database systems typically refer to indexing as the creation of a secondary data structure such as B-tree on top of a table attribute for faster searching. In this context, indexing refers to building an inverted index on top of the given dataset.

Consider a thick book for which a sequential search (line by line) for a specific combination of terms is impossible. For example, in a children's bedtime stories book, we might search for the following: all stories containing the words "sunshine" and "candies" and not containing the word "ghosts."

From an IR system perspective, the query can be shown as follows:

sunshine AND candies AND NOT ghosts

The following sections discuss the ways in which this query can be executed.

Linear Scan

A *linear scan* is a simple process of sequentially going through each line in the system and checking for the parameters (i.e., conditions in the given query). This is precisely how Unix's grep command works, and it also works fairly well with wildcards and regular expressions. If the size of data set being searched size is not too large and the hardware being used is reasonably powerful, linear search is the simplest way.

However, linear search starts showing performance degradations beyond a million medium-sized documents. The world around us is experiencing an information explosion. In fact, the amount of data that needs to be processed to extract relevant information has quadrupled over the last 10 years, thanks to the advent of connected world, hand held devices and IoT. Linear search cannot scale to meet those needs, and so we need something more sophisticated and performant that can handle massive datasets while still providing relevant results at reasonable speeds.

Linear searches also limit what kind of queries can be answered. For example, there is no way to define a query that seeks "close" matches of a given pattern. Suppose, for instance, that we search for documents with the words "flower" and "sunshine" within a proximity of three words in a document. Doing so with linear search is impossible. Also, there is no notion of ranked results. That is, given a query, a result is either a match or not for a linear scan. If we want some sort of ranking, we cannot use a linear scan.

An *inverted index* is a data structure used to store data in an "inverted" manner (i.e., terms are mapped to documents in which the terms appear). Any unique term appearing in any document is made a part of the inverted index.

As shown in Figure 1-1, this data structure proves useful for answering questions like "find me the documents containing Term1" in an optimized manner. As you can see, a single-term search is a constant-time operation.

Term	Document IDs
Term1	Book1
Term2	Book1, Book2
Term3	Book1, Book2
Term4	Book2
Term6	Book3

Book1	Book2	Book3
Term1	Term 2	Term6
Term2	Term3	
Term3	Term4	

Figure 1-1. *A Representation of Inverted Index*

To create an inverted index, the fields within the document are first split and tokenized, a sorted list of all the unique terms is created, and the documents that contain the corresponding terms are populated.

While being fast for a single-term query, inverted indexes can also answer an important class of questions: similarity queries.

Figure 1-2 shows the typical way a query is processed in IR systems. A query comes in and is parsed and split into individual tokens. A token is an independent term having its own semantics in a query.

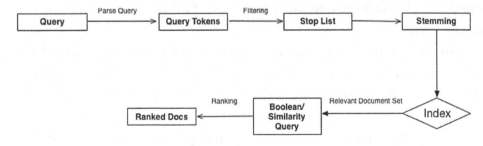

Figure 1-2. *Control Flow of Query Process*

For example, consider the following query:

> Find all people who drove to college yesterday

In this scenario, tokenizing the query will lead to independent terms such as "drove," "college," "yesterday," and "to."

Stop List

A *stop list* consists of words that are used in the associated language to form the structure of sentences but are not necessarily useful for semantic matching and searching. For example, in the sentence "Alex went to London," we see that the word "to" is a stop word because that helps form the structure of the query. However, it cannot necessarily contribute anything to the semantic assessment of a potential document match, and so it should not be considered on the same lines.

Stop words are filtered out before further processing to help limit the number of tokens in the index to the ones that can contribute to the relevance of the document. Of course, later on, we might discover that some of the semantically-able words are not useful in matching relevant documents, but that is done stage by stage, and we do not want to overoptimize.

Stemming

Queries can contain words in different forms, with different tenses, spellings, and associated grammatical semantics. For example, "drive," "driving," and "drives" are all based on the same word but differ in their structure. However, for semantic matching, the actual structure of the word is of little value. What really matters is the root word, which will contribute to calculating the overall relevance of a document to the query.

Another advantage of discounting different structures of the same word is to allow one to match the remaining. For example, a query containing the word "drive" should match documents containing the word "driving." This increases the *recall* of the query results. Recall is defined as the breadth of the returned results (i.e., how many documents match a given query). Unlike a relational database, IR systems can answer queries with a semantic element with them; that is, any document can match the given query. The trick is to identify the most relevant ones and eliminate the unnecessary noise.

Note   *Recall* is the width of documents in the returned results. However, too high a recall, and the returned results will have lower correctness. Too low a recall, and the returned results are very small in size. Most IR systems struggle with this trade-off.

Stemming is the process of reducing words to their base word and removing the structural differences between words that originate from the same root. However, stemming can be crude in its operations. For example, stemming can employ a crude heuristic to remove parts of words, which can sometimes lead to weird semantic outputs. While this is efficient and works most of the time, a more sophisticated way to deal with this requirement is the art of lemmatization: rewriting words using a given vocabulary and depending on morphological analysis of the tokens of the query. Lemmatization is beyond the scope of the current discussion.

To avoid linear search, you can index the set of documents in advance and use special queries to get the right set of results. Consider, for instance, a set of documents with a range of words present. Let's use a group of related books, as shown here:

> Databases in Action World of Lucene Introduction
> to Information Retrieval

Let's now assume that we have to serve queries across all three of these books. Doing so requires that we index data across all three books so that we can be efficient in query operations. Note that there are multiple ways to do the same thing. We can create a separate index per book, or index all three books in the same index. To see what kind of index are we building, refer back to Figure 1-1.

Note that these books will have some key terms in common. For example, we expect "search" to be present across all three of the texts. Similarly, "bytes" is another term that can repeat across all three texts.

A naive indexing technique is to maintain independent metadata about each of the documents, effectively discarding the common terms present. This method is a waste of space, and is also inefficient for serving queries that seek matches across all the texts.

To implement inverted indexes as outlined in Figure 1-1, you first need to understand the concepts of a term and a term-document incidence matrix.

Term

A *term* is an independent indexable unit in an IR system. Terms are generally words, but they can be more complex and structured types as well. Examples pertaining to our data set are "search" and "bytes."

Term-Document Incidence Matrix

A *term-document incidence matrix* is what maps a term to the documents that hold the given term. Simply put, it is a two-dimensional matrix, where the column represents the name of the book, and the row represents the terms involved.

Figure 1-3 shows a term-incidence matrix for a given set of books and terms.

	Book1	Book2
"Bytes"	1	1
"Term"	0	1
"Index"	1	1
"Result"	1	0
"Error"	1	1

Figure 1-3. *Term Incidence Matrix*

Serving Queries Using a Term-Document Incidence Matrix

This section explains how to serve queries using the built structure. A simple model using a term-document incidence matrix involves building vectors for queries being served. For example, consider a query:

> TERM and INDEX and not RESULT

Using the vectors for each of the associated terms, we perform the following:

> vector(term) AND vector(index) AND NOT
> vector(result)

The AND NOT vector(result) can be converted into AND ~vector(result), where ~ represent the complement of the boolean vector.

This converts to the following:

vector(term) AND vector(index) AND ~vector(result)

Replacing with actual boolean vectors

01 AND 11 AND 10

yields the final result of the query: Book2.

Now that you have a basic understanding of how inverted indexes work, are built, and are used for querying, let's take a look at actual Lucene implementations.

Basic Terminology

Before discussing the finer aspects of Lucene's data structures, here are some general terms you want to understand. These terms will help you navigate your journey through Lucene:

- *Document*: A record; the unit of search; the thing returned as search results

- *Field*: A typed slot in a document for storing and indexing values

- *Index*: A collection of documents, typically with the same schema

- *Corpus*: The entire set of documents in an index

- *Inverted index*: Internal data structure that maps terms to documents by a unique identifier.

- *Term*: Value extracted from source document, used for building the inverted index

- *Vocabulary*: The full set of distinct terms in a corpus

- *Field data*: Array of all field values per field, sorted by document identifiers

- *Doc values*: Columnar store representing field values

Heart of Lucene's Data Representation

Note that at its most basic, Lucene stores data in the form of an inverted index, similar to what we discussed earlier. However, the actual representation, construction, and storage of the inverted index are optimized and specific for Lucene, as discussed next.

Lucene's Inverted Index Structure

Before looking closer at the semantics of this format, let's first review some basic elements of Lucene's indexing and searching terminology:

- *Term*: Term in Lucene is the equivalent of a token in the English language, only much more powerful and semantically augmented than its English language counterpart. Terms can be analyzed or not analyzed in Lucene, although non-analyzed terms hold little value. Consider the following input to Lucene:

"Foo" : "Bar"

This converts into the term "Bar" and is queryable in that format by any such Lucene queries.

Remember that a term is the basic unit of both indexing and search. Lucene stores its underlying data as terms, and user queries are deconstructed into terms and then sent for further processing.

- *Term dictionary*: A term dictionary is what holds the terms indexed in the Lucene index and their corresponding document frequencies.

On-Disk Representation of a Lucene Index

The on-disk representation of a Lucene index is optimized to be efficient in reads and writes, and it allows searches into required areas of the index.

At the heart of Lucene lies the Lucene index file format. Post Lucene 4, formats are pluggable (using custom codecs, as discussed later in this chapter). However, the default file format is what is published on Lucene's official website and what this section covers.

Referring to Figure 1-4, the basic components to start defining are as follows:

- *Field definition*: Field definitions are stored in an independent file named FieldInfos (with the extension .fnm).

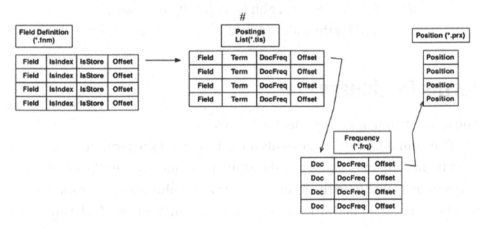

Figure 1-4. *Lucene Index Structure*

From the official definition:

FieldInfos (.fnm) --> FNMVersion,FieldsCount, <FieldName, FieldBits> FieldsCount

> FNMVersion, FieldsCount --> VInt
>
> FieldName --> Strings
>
> FieldBits --> Byte
>
> The low-order bit is one for indexed fields, and zero for nonindexed fields.
>
> The second lowest-order bit is one for fields that have term vectors stored, and zero for fields without term vectors.
>
> If the third lowest-order bit is set (0x04), term positions are stored with the term vectors.
>
> If the fourth lowest-order bit is set (0x08), term offsets are stored with the term vectors.
>
> If the fifth lowest-order bit is set (0x10), norms are omitted for the indexed field.
>
> If the sixth lowest-order bit is set (0x20), payloads are stored for the indexed field.

Terms Dictionary

The terms dictionary is represented by two files:

The term infos (or tis) file holds metadata about the term, such as term name, skip information, and document frequency (i.e., the count of documents that hold the term). A tis file also holds useful information that helps Lucene build structures for more optimal access of relevant documents for a given term (Lucene uses skip data structures internally to make access faster, and the tis file holds data to help build this structure.) In addition, metadata such as term frequencies in this file allows faster access in other files.

The term infos index file (extension .tii) holds metadata to allow random access to the term infos file.

Frequencies File

The frequencies file (extension .frq) maps documents to a term. That is, it contains a list of all documents that contain a term present in the terms dictionary, along with the frequency of each term in the document.

Positions File

The positions file (extension .prx) represents the list of positions at which each term occurs within documents.

Queries on Lucene

Queries are the life and soul of how applications interact and extract data from Lucene.

Lucene has multiple core capabilities on this front and allows rich and semantically diverse queries to be built. One key feature in Lucene's query engine is the extensibility and the ability to set custom parameters to customize search and ranking according to the user's desire, as discussed in later chapters.

Contrary to common expectations, Lucene does not support SQL or SQL-ish syntax. Lucene has a custom query syntax designed to make the best use of all that Lucene has to offer.

Structure of a Lucene Query

Lucene's queries consist of two principal parts: terms and operators. Because we have discussed the definition and semantic relevance of terms earlier, there is no need to details that again here. However, two important categorizations of terms will prove useful for our further discussion:

- *Single terms*: Single terms are terms that consist of a single token (e.g., "walk"). They are generally atomic and constitute the fundamental construct of a query.

- *Phrases*: Phrases are a multiterm phenomenon consisting of groups of single terms. An example is "Walk This Way." A phrase allows richer query matching and retrieval and a more semantically powerful way to express queries. Table 1-1 gives a description of the queries and their equivalent applications and a sample query for each.

Table 1-1.

Query	Application	Sample Query
TermQuery	Single-term match	"Foo":"Bar"
PhraseQuery	Several terms Coupled together	"All Cars With Black Tyres"
RangeQuery	Range of terms, excluding or including the endpoints	"AGE":[13-19]
PrefixQuery	Matches given prefix	Foo*
FuzzyQuery	Levenshtein algorithm for closeness matching	Foo~
WildcardQuery	Regular expression Like matching	F??bar
BooleanQuery	Multiple queries connected by logical clauses	"NAME:Ramesh" AND "AGE":[13-19]

Fields

Fields are used to specify predicates when defining a query. Fields are data corpus specific and can be used during query construction. Any valid field that is queryable can be specified upon. When performing a search, you can specify the field in which you want to search. You can use any existing field name as a field name. You can specify multiple fields in some types of queries.

Types of Queries in Lucene

This section covers the different query types available in Lucene, their applications, and a short example.

Figure 1-5 shows a way to instantiate a composite query and set a set of clauses in it. Most queries support a single predicate, but some queries, such as BooleanQuery, support multiple and diverse clauses, thus allowing for more complex search.

```
1
2    public void queryExample throws Exception {
3      BooleanQuery exampleQuery = new BooleanQuery();
4      exampleQuery.add(new TermQuery(new Term("foo",
   "bar")), Occur.MUST);
5      exampleQuery.add(new TermQuery(new Term("foo2",
   "bar2")), Occur.SHOULD);
6      exampleQuery.add(new TermQuery(new Term("foo3",
   "bar3")), Occur.MUST_NOT);
7
```

Figure 1-5.

17

Lucene vs. Relational Databases

Although similar in many ways, IR systems differ inherently from traditional relational database systems. Key differences include the following:

- Databases offer the strictness of schemas, thus enforcing that the data fed to the system is cast in a specific structure. IR systems, in contrast, tend to be schema-less and work on a tuple-based model.

- Databases, building on top of schemas, allow data modeling (such as an entity relationship diagram). IR systems do not have that capability (and neither do they need it).

- Databases have to be queried with precise values, but IR systems allow imprecise search and semantics.

- Databases are typically used for precise and exact retrievals, whereas IR systems are normally used for imprecise and "wide" searches, where all documents can match a query, and hence the concepts of ranking and relevance apply.

CHAPTER 2

Hello World: The Lucene Way

This chapter covers indexing data with Lucene, specifically how Lucene stores and represents data, Lucene query nuances, and how Lucene facilitates multiparameter search.

Indexing Data in Lucene

IndexWriter is the main user-facing class responsible for indexing data in Lucene. IndexWriter is used for analyzing documents, opening directories, and writing the data to directories.

Figure 2-1 shows the overall flow of an indexing operation. A document consisting of various fields is first passed to the analyzer, after which it is given to an IndexWriter instance. IndexWriter interacts with the internals of Lucene to open the relevant directory, forms the index in the correct and required format, and writes the same to the underlying directory. Any readers opened after this have access (visibility) to that document.

© Atri Sharma 2020
A. Sharma, *Practical Apache Lucene 8*, https://doi.org/10.1007/978-1-4842-6345-7_2

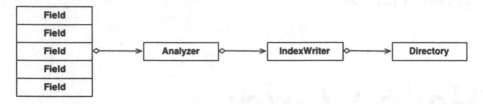

Figure 2-1. *Flow of an indexing operation*

Let's now take a closer look at the classes involved in this process.

Document

Document is the base class representing a document and its associated contents in Lucene. A document is the macro unit for both indexing and search; both indexing and search process data in document units.

A Document consists of one or more instances of the Field class. A field is a combination of a key and a value. A field can be stored or not. A stored field is returned with search hits, and so ideally each document should contain at least one stored field. However, stored fields can significantly add to the storage footprint of the index. In worst cases (where all fields are stored), field storage can lead to an increase of about 30% in the overall storage size of the on-disk index.

When you create a Document class' instance, you can mark each field as analyzed or not. A field marked as analyzed is run through an analyzer.

Analyzers

Analyzers analyze data before it that data is passed as input to another Lucene class. You can use analyzers for both indexing and searching, and their use is generally recommended. Analyzers typically split the input text into tokens, using a set of tokenizers already defined and applying a set of filters. The following sections cover a few of the available analyzers in Lucene.

StandardAnalyzer

Most Lucene users use StandardAnalyzer, a one-size-fits-all analyzer designed for simplicity, generic behavior, and ease of use.

StandardAnalyzer removes stop words from the input, which is a great help when processing naturally occurring text. StandardAnalyzer also converts text to lowercase (an important point to note because case issues can lead to subtle bugs in application code when searching for data indexed with StandardAnalyzer).

Note   StandardAnalyzer lowercases data. So, remember this and ensure that you use the same analyzer while searching or converting the text to lowercase yourself.

Here is an example:

- *Input:* "Lucene Is A Library"

- *Output:* [Lucene] [a] [Library]

StopAnalyzer

StopAnalyzer is similar to StandardAnalyzer, but it performs stop-word removal using the StopFilter.

SimpleAnalyzer

SimpleAnalyzer is again similar to StandardAnalyzer, but it cannot remove stop words and cannot recognize URLs.

Here is an example:

- *Input:* "Lucene Is A Library"

- *Output:* [Lucene] [is] [a] [Library]

The following code sample shows an input analyzer used to analyze a piece of text and return a tokenized result. Note that the tokenized result depends on the analyzer being used and the characteristics of the analyzer:

```
public List<String> performAnalyze(String input, Analyzer
analyser) throws IOException {
        List<String> result = new ArrayList<String>();
        TokenStream tokenStream = analyser.tokenStream("field_
        name", input);
        CharTermAttribute attr = tokenStream.
        addAttribute(CharTermAttribute.class);
        tokenStream.reset();
        while(tokenStream.incrementToken()) {
                result.add(attracts.toString());
        }
        return result;
}
```

IndexWriter

IndexWriter creates and writes data to an index. Because IndexWriter is a crucial component of the indexing process, users building applications need to understand it.

IndexWriter enables you to both create a new index and open an existing index. Remember that Lucene indexes are append only. That is, once data is written, it is immutable until a process known as segment merging (discussed later) merges older data. This immutability allows an

IndexWriter to work on existing indexes that currently just serve queries. The currently running queries just use a snapshot of the index and do not interfere in the IndexWriter's data-writing process.

IndexWriter supports a diverse set of application programming interfaces (APIs) to interact with the underlying data and to allow complex and custom interactions with the data. New documents can be added with addDocument(), documents can be deleted with deleteDocuments(), and an existing document can be updated with updateDocument(). Note that deleteDocuments() can be passed in a query as well, and all documents matching the query will be deleted. Updating a document implies a delete and an insert because Lucene indexes are append only.

IndexWriter writes data to a new segment within the index. A segment is a logical unit of data within a Lucene index. Calling commit() forces the creation of a new segment. However, calling commit() after each document insertion is an expensive operation and a bad idea. Note that commit() is an atomic operation.

Directory

Directory represents the logical representation of a filesystem-level directory. Directory allows creation and access of indexes and supports random accesses. Lucene supports a variety of Directory implementations, such as one using Java's Non-blocking I/O (NIO) (NIOFSDirectory), another one that MMaps files (MMapDirectory), and so forth.

Let's now create documents and index them with the following high-level steps:

1. Create documents.

2. Create index and open it for writing.

3. Index data.

Create Documents

For this example, assume that we get a File instance as the input. We then complete the following steps:

1. Get fields from the raw File instance.

2. Create Lucene Field instances from the data you get in step 1.

3. Set relevant properties for each field.

4. Create a Lucene document.

5. Add the fields to the document.

The following code follows the above steps in given order:

```
private Document parseAndCreateDocument(File file) throws
IOException {
//Assume we have a parser that returns different fields from
the file
FancyParser fancyParser = FancyParser.getParser().parse(file);

//Step 1
String firstTest = fancyParser.getFirst();
String secondText = fancyParser.getSecond();
String thirdText = fancyParser.getThird();

//Steps 2 and 3
Field firstField = new Field("first_field", firstText, Field.
Store.YES, Field.Index.NOT_ANALYZED);
Field secondField = new Field("second_field", secondText,
Field.Store.YES, Field.Index.NOT_ANALYZED);
Field thirdField = new Field("third_field", thirdText, Field.
Store.YES, Field.Index.NOT_ANALYZED);

//Step 4
Document document = new Document();
```

```
//Step 5
document.add(firstField);
document.add(secondField);
document.add(thirdField);

return document;
}
```

Create Index and Write Documents

In this section, we create a new index and use it to index documents. As described earlier, the main components involved in this process are IndexWriter and Directory. IndexWriter enables both creation of the index and writing to the index. IndexWriter uses a directory below it to actually write the needed data.

The high-level steps are as follows:

1. Create an IndexWriter instance.

2. Create a Lucene directory in which to storage the index.

3. Initialize the IndexWriter with the correct configuration.

Implementing the above steps:

```
public IndexWriter getIndexWriter(String path) throws
IOException {
        //Step 1
        IndexWriter indexWriter;

        //Step 2
        FSDirectory.open(new File(path));

        //Step 3
        indexWriter = new IndexWriter(indexDirectory,
```

```
                            new StandardAnalyzer(Version.
                            LUCENE_80), true,
                            IndexWriter.MaxFieldLength.UNLIMITED);

        return indexWriter;
}
```

Adding Data to the Index

You can add data to the index just created in a number of ways. Note that
IndexWriter is not just used to create but also to add/delete and update
documents in the index. The analyzer passed in as a parameter during creation
of an IndexWriter instance determines how the input documents are analyzed
before they are added to the index. The following code shows a simple example
of an IndexWriter instance writing a document into its corresponding index:

```
private void doIndexing(File file, IndexWriter indexWriter)
throws IOException {
        //Check that the indexWriter is not null and is open
        if (indexWriter == null) {
                throw new IllegalArgumentsException("IndexWriter
                instance must not be null");
        }

        if (!indexWriter.isOpen()) {
                throw new IllegalArgumentsException("IndexWriter
                instance must be open");
        }

        Document document = parseAndCreateDocument(file);

        indexWriter.addDocument(document);
}
```

Bringing It All Together

Here is the final class with all components:

```
public class DemoIndexing {
  private final String indexPath;
  public Indexer(String indexDirectoryPath) throws IOException
{
    this.indexPath = indexDirectoryPath;
  }

  private Document parseAndCreateDocument(File file) throws
  IOException {
    Document document = new Document();
    //Assume we have a parser that returns different
    //fields from the file
    FancyParser fancyParser = FancyParser.getParser().parse(file);
    String        firstText   = fancyParser.getFirst();
    String        secondText  = fancyParser.getSecond();
    String        thirdText   = fancyParser.getThird();

    Field firstField = new Field("first_field", firstText,
      Field.Store.YES,Field.Index.NOT_ANALYZED);
    Field secondField = new Field("second_field", secondText,
      Field.Store.YES,Field.Index.NOT_ANALYZED);
    Field thirdField = new Field("third_field", thirdText,
      Field.Store.YES,Field.Index.NOT_ANALYZED);
    document.add(firstField);
    document.add(secondField);
    document.add(thirdField);

    return document;
  }
}
```

```java
public IndexWriter getIndexWriter(String path) throws
IOException {
    IndexWriter indexWriter;
    Directory indexDirectory = FSDirectory.open(new File(path));

    //Create the indexer
    indexWriter = new IndexWriter(indexDirectory,
      new StandardAnalyzer(Version.LUCENE_80),true,
      IndexWriter.MaxFieldLength.UNLIMITED);
    return indexWriter;
}

    private void doIndexing(File file, IndexWriter indexWriter)
    throws IOException {
      //Check that the indexWriter is not null and is open
      if (indexWriter == null) {
        throw new IllegalArgumentsException("IndexWriter
        instance must not be null");
      }
      if (!indexWriter.isOpen() {
        throw new IllegalArgumentsException("IndexWriter
        instance must be open");
      }
      //Get the document using the method we wrote earlier
      Document document = parseAndCreateDocument(file);
      writer.addDocument(document);
  }

  public void index(List<File> files) {
    IndexWriter indexWriter = getIndexWriter(indexPath);
    for (File file : files) {
```

```
        doIndexing(file, indexWriter);
    }
  }
}
```

TestClass

The following TestClass demonstrates a class's functionality:

```
public class TestClass {
        DemoIndexer demoIndexer;
        List<Files> files;

        public TestClass(List<Files> files) {
                this.files = files;
        }

        public static void main(String[] args) {
                //args[0] is the directory name
                try {
                        index();
                } catch (IOException e) {
                        e.printStackTrace();
                }
        }

        private void index() throws IOException {
                demoIndexer.index(files);
        }
}
```

Let's now take a look at how to query the data we just wrote to the index.

Document Search

The Lucene search API takes a query and optionally a number of top hits to return. The documents to be returned are ordered by relevance and score. The score represents the "closeness" of the hit to the given parameters. The next chapter discusses Lucene ranking and scoring models. The following code executes a search and returns top N hits.

```
private void performIndexSearch(File indexDir, String query,
int maxHits) throws Exception {
        Directory directory = FSDirectory.open(indexDir);
        //Contents is the default field to be analyzed
        QueryParser parser = new QueryParser(Version.LUCENE_80,
        "contents', new StandardAnalyzer());
        Query query = parser.parse(query);
        TopDocs topDocs = searcher.search(query. maxHits);

        //Get the top documents that were returned for this
        //query (specified by maxHits)
        ScoreDoc[] hits = topDocs.scoreDocs;

        for (int i = 0; i < hits.length; i++) {
                int docId = hits[I].doc;
                System.out.println(docId);
        }
}
```

Let's now look at specifics of the code.

Directory is the underlying implementation that allows accessing, loading, and reading the index being searched.

QueryParser

QueryParser generates a Query instance out of a query string. A query can consist of a family of clauses. A clause can be prefixed by + or -, indicating that the clause is MUST or MUST_NOT. as the preceding code shows, the constructor invoked defines the codec to be used (LUCENE_80), the default field ("contents") and the analyzer to be used (StandardAnalyzer()).

TopDocs

TopDocs is the representation of the top documents that match the given query. They are a generic representation and do not necessarily depend on the underlying algorithm used to calculate how the top documents are calculated. TopDocs consist of two components: scoreDocs (the documentIDs of the top N hits, where N was the requested value) and the score of each of those hits. The score of a document is an Lucene internal concept discussed later in this chapter.

The second part of TopDocs is totalHits, which represents the total number of hits.

In the preceding code sample, we get TopDocs by specifying the query and the number of hits we want returned.

IndexSearcher

IndexSearcher is the abstraction present in Lucene that executes search over a single Lucene index. IndexSearcher is opened on top of IndexReader, which is used to read the underlying index using the Directory and corresponding abstractions. Note that we need IndexReader since the Directory might represent the index in a format that is not immediately useful for searching (hence the need for an abstraction to deal with the scenario).

31

IndexSearcher instances are expensive to build and so should be reused unless the underlying index changes and the user wants to see the updated values. The reuse can be done by reopening the searcher with DirectoryReader.openIfChanged(DirectoryReader). The constructor used in the preceding code opens an IndexSearcher with the given directory.

IndexReader

IndexReader is an abstraction provided to allow an interface to access an index. The two types of IndexReader are as follows:

- AtomicReader: These readers read actual files such as postings, doc values, terms, and stored fields. These operations are atomic.

- CompositeReader: CompositeReader instances are used to get stored fields from underlying AtomicReaders. Note that it is not possible to directly get a postings list from CompositeReader instances; you still need to get the underlying AtomicReader instances.

Searching

At the core of Lucene's information-retrieval mechanism lies the scoring algorithms that determine the relevance of a document to the given query.

Let's first look at the query-execution model that Lucene uses.

Boolean Model

In the boolean model, a query is expressed as a family of AND, OR, and NOT connected predicates to find the documents that match a query.

For example, the query x AND y AND z will only match documents that have x and y and z present.

What Is Relevance?

Relevance refers to the measure of similarity (that is, how relevant a document is to a given query). Each document is assigned a score that is used to filter documents out and return top hits (see Figure 2-2). Note that relevance is calculated per query for all documents.

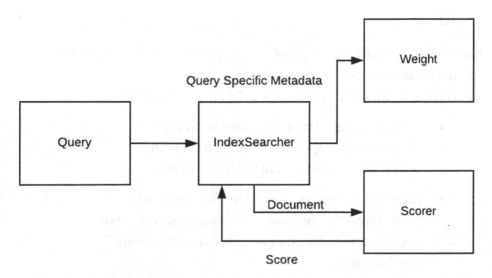

Figure 2-2. *Search layout*

Following the boolean model described earlier, let's assume that the query consists of multiple clauses, each of which can be the same or different.

Each clause contributes to the scoring differently, and not all clauses necessarily contribute to scoring.

Note that the parameters for relevance (or similarity) as seen by each type of query are different.

33

Scoring Algorithms

Scoring algorithms are what determine the "similarity" of documents given a query (that is, how close a given document is to the given query).

Lucene has a number of scoring algorithms. The following subsections describe the most common ones.

TF/IDF

Term frequency/inverse document frequency (TF/IDF) is the default scoring algorithm Lucene uses.

The following factors contribute to TF/IDF's scoring model:

- *Term frequency*: Term frequency is simply the frequency of a repetition rate of a term in the document. A repetition of 5 is better than 1.

- *Inverse document frequency*: Inverse document frequency is the measure of how frequently the term appears across documents. This defines the "rare" words from the

- "common." For example, if a word occurs only in one document, that might be a more interesting hit than some word that occurs in 80% of the documents.

- *Field length norm*: Field length is an important aspect of measuring the relevance of a term and a hit document. The longer the matched field, the lesser the probability of the field being only about the term. The shorter the field, the higher the probability.

These three factors in conjunction generate a weight that signals the significance of the document.

Vector Space Model

The Vector Space Model uses a vector model to compare against multiple terms in a query. Every term in the vector represents the TF/IDF score of one term of the query. Note that TF/IDF is one option. Any other scoring model can also be used here.

Consider a query for "foo bar," for example. For this query, calculate the weight of each term for each document, construct a vector for each document, and plot them with the vector for the query. The angle between the vectors gives the deviation or, conversely, the relevance.

Scoring Example

Consider a document containing 100 words wherein the word "cat" appears 3 times. The term frequency (tf) for "cat" is then (3 / 100) = 0.03. Now, assume we have 10 million documents, and the word "cat" appears in 1,000 of these. Then, the inverse document frequency (idf) is calculated as log(10,000,000 / 1,000) = 4. Therefore, the tf-idf weight is the product of these quantities: 0.03 * 4 = 0.12.

Lucene's Scoring Model

Whereas single-term queries are good for learning and their internals, real production workloads deal with multiterm queries. Lucene builds a model combining all of what was discussed earlier in this chapter into a single generic model.

Lucene's core querying model is built on a boolean model; all multiterm queries are a family of clauses connected by predicates.

The core idea for Lucene's scoring algorithm is that it takes stock of the number of times a term appears in a document relative to the number of times the term appears in all documents in the said collection. If a document has 100 occurrences of the term, and the times the term appears in all documents is 10,000, that is a worse score than when a term appears 5 times in a document and 7 times across all documents in the collection.

Fields

Fields are the building blocks of documents. Documents consist of a set of fields. Note that Lucene's scoring works on fields and not documents, so field representations are crucial in the way scores are computed.

Similarity

The Similarity class is what is responsible for the final "closeness" computation for a given term. Similarity can be overridden, and advanced users can write their own similarity. However, those are tricky waters to chart, so caution is advised.

Once the boolean clauses identified for filtering terms are used to approve documents, they are then scored using the Similarity class defined. The default scoring model works on TF/IDF and computes results that are then returned upstream for further processing.

Boosting

Boosting can be done at three levels:

- *Document-level boosting:* Can be specified at index time

- *Field-level boosting:* Can be specified at the time of adding the field to the document

- *Query level boosting:* Can be specified during querying by specifying boost on a specific clause in the query

Boosts allow influencing the entire scoring decision and giving priorities to a specific document, field, or clause in a query.

Collectors

Collectors are the "file vault" of querying in Lucene. They collect hits as dictated by the given query. Collectors are very useful because they define the structure of results and can be used to process hits in a much more helpful manner. Examples include top-score docs collectors (described in the next section), elastic search aggregations, and so on.

Users can write their custom collectors by implementing the `Collector` interface defined in Lucene. This facility allows for great flexibility in terms of what can be done with hits collected and how hits are returned/ranked.

In most common search cases, the user cares only about the top N relevant hits for a given query and dataset. Top N query supported in Lucene is useful for building search engines, searching for items, and so on.

Lucene provides a special mechanism to serve this exact specific set of queries. These are known as top N hits queries.

Typically, a user must specify a `Collector` and a `Query` to the underlying `IndexSearcher` to get the query to populate the results needed. However, for the top N hits, the user can specify the query and the number of hits requested, and Lucene will internally create a `Collector` from a family of collectors (known as `TopScoreDocsCollector`) and return an object of a class named `TopDocs`. TopDocs is responsible for holding the top N hits of the given query.

Internally, `TopScoreDocCollector` uses a priority queue to maintain documents according to their score. When the collection completes, the priority queue is used to return the top N hits.

CHAPTER 3

Core Search Fundamentals

Queries are the fundamental building blocks in any application using Lucene, and so they should be. After all, Lucene is much loved because of its powerful search capabilities built on top of its sophisticated indexing models.

This chapter covers Lucene core search fundamentals, the components involved in the process, and the more commonly used constructs used to tap into the power of Lucene search.

As an overview, this chapter introduces you to the basics without delving too deeply into complex details.

Codecs

Codecs enable the reading and writing of indexes.

Lucene defines an abstract class, Codec, which outlines the contract that users of Codec should be expecting as the model of usage. Each physical codec needs to implement the contract and ensure that it is as performant as possible. (Remember that codecs are generally actively used in the critical path of indexing, so any performance leaks there can impact the overall performance of index creation/updating/deletion.)

A salient aspect of Codec is that it abstracts the complexity and low-level details of how an index is stored. Recall from earlier chapters that Lucene

© Atri Sharma 2020
A. Sharma, *Practical Apache Lucene 8*, https://doi.org/10.1007/978-1-4842-6345-7_3

represents its indexes in a multifaceted manner, with quite a bit of low-level tuning to ensure that the corresponding read and write operations are fast. In this way, Lucene allows a wide variety of operations to be performed easily on the data structures. Codecs honor that promise while hiding the specific details from the user.

The abstract representation also ensures flexibility to change the underlying implementation of the codec without any user breakage, because all codecs must implement the same contract.

A codec returns a concrete instance of the Format class for different types of components of the underlying index.

Format implementations used/returned by Codec include the following:

- StoredFieldsFormat: Represents the fields stored in the underlying index

- FieldsInfoFormat: Has the per-field metadata

- PostingsFormat: Represents the underlying postings list, including fields, terms, documents, offsets, and so on

- DocValuesFormat: Represents the columnar store (used for operations like grouping, range queries, and sorted access)

A new type of format, CompoundFormat, is used when compound indexes are enabled. Traditionally, Lucene stores the different layouts within its index in different files on disk. However, in newer versions of Lucene, compound indexes can be turned on, leading to a singular representation of the physical files of the index (and leading to codecs returning CompoundFormat, which enables accessing the same).

DocValues

Lucene uses its inverted index functionality to store data in an inverted format and allow matching queries to generate results. However, this way of doing things limits Lucene's ability to perform other interesting stuff. For example, if we want to group by a field, or sort, or facet, inverted indexes cannot provide this functionality.

Lucene has an important component for solving this specific use case: DocValues. DocValues are a columnar store, an uninverted form of the inverted index. Specifically, DocValues allow access to specific fields. All the values associated with a field are colocated, making accesses efficient.

One common argument in that direction is that stored fields provide similar functionality (i.e., accessing specific values for fields). However, stored fields work best when their data is bulk loaded into the system's memory. They are not optimal for point seeks in the field's values.

Think of DocValues as an inverted index that reverse maps what Lucene's regular inverted index maps. (That is, DocValues map document IDs to field values.) Storing field values in a colocated manner also helps with disk reads, because reads typically happen in blocks (and hence colocated values will most likely be loaded when a block from a disk is read into main memory). In this scenario, further seeks should have a much lower latency because ideally the data should already be present in the memory.

To think about uses, consider a scenario in which a field is being used for sorting hits identified by the scoring criteria. To sort, we need actual field values. One way to do this is to do a document read using the document ID of the hit, and you then use the necessary field/fields to get the needed values.

However, this method is inefficient and a performance unworthy for this type of queries. The optimal way to execute such queries is to have a columnar store that maps document IDs to field values, giving all the benefits described earlier. So, the value of using DocValues should be obvious to you now.

You can add a DocValue to a document as follows:

```
doc.add(new SortedDocValuesField ("date", new BytesRef(date) ));
```

Phrase Queries

Phrase queries are used to match "phrases" of terms. A group of terms given in a sequence are searched, and documents maintaining that sequence are then returned, as follows:

```
private void searchPhraseQuery(String[] phrases)
  throws IOException, ParseException {

  searcher = new Searcher(indexDir);
  long startTime = System.currentTimeMillis();
  PhraseQuery query = new PhraseQuery();
  query.setSlop(0);

  for(String word:phrases) {
    query.add(new Term(LuceneConstants.FILE_NAME,word));
  }

  TopDocs hits = searcher.search(query);
  long endTime = System.currentTimeMillis();

  for(ScoreDoc scoreDoc : hits.scoreDocs) {
    Document doc = searcher.getDocument(scoreDoc);
    System.out.println("File: "+ doc.get(LuceneConstants.FILE_PATH));
  }
  searcher.close();
}
```

Phrase queries mandate that the given terms occur in any document in sequence. For example, "hi friend" as a phrase needs to match "hi" and "friend," and "friend" needs to immediately succeed "hi."

You can lift this restriction, however, by giving a value for the slop parameter. The slop parameter allows N number of words to occur between words in the phrase for a document to match. The higher the value of slop, the more the number of hits. (A higher value might not necessarily be a good idea, though, because a high value of slop can lead to unnecessary noise in the returned documents.)

Term Vectors

As you may recall, a term is the basic searchable unit in Lucene. It consists of a pair of strings, the field name, and the value.

Term vectors are a field-level data structure that are useful for a wide variety of operations. If a term vector is enabled for a field, all terms in the field will be present in the term vector, and the corresponding metadata will be computed for each term.

Let's take a look at a couple of use cases to understand the value of term vectors.

Consider a case in which a user wants to mine similarity between two documents, or wants to get a preview of a data field from the hits given by a query. In both scenarios, the underlying task is to get extra metadata about hits once a query generates the corresponding hits.

This kind of operation is hard in an inverted index because the structure and layout of inverted indexes do not allow easy fetching of content around a hit. To solve that specific issue, term vectors come to the rescue.

We can use term vectors to get such data and to perform complex ranking (such as in the Vector Space Model), or similarity ranking, or just to get a text summary from a hit.

```
RAMDirectory ramDir = new RAMDirectory();
//Index some made-up content
```

```
IndexWriter writer = new IndexWriter(ramDir, new
StandardAnalyzer(), true,
  IndexWriter.MaxFieldLength.UNLIMITED);

for (int i = 0; i < DOCS.length; i++){
  Document doc = new Document();
  Field id = new Field("id", "doc_" + i, Field.Store.YES,
    Field.Index.NOT_ANALYZED_NO_NORMS);
  doc.add(id);

  //Store both position and offset information
  Field text = new Field("content", DOCS[i], Field.Store.NO,
Field.Index.ANALYZED,
    Field.TermVector.WITH_POSITIONS_OFFSETS);
  doc.add(text);
  writer.addDocument(doc);
}
writer.close();
```

Think of term vectors as micro inverted indexes against a single document. The various modes of term vector construction include the following:

- TermVector.YES: Only store the number of occurrences.

- TermVector.WITH_POSITIONS: Store the number of occurrence and positions of terms, but no offset.

- TermVector.WITH_OFFSETS: Store the number of occurrence and offsets of terms, but no positions.

- TermVector.WITH_POSITIONS_OFFSETS: Store the number of occurrence and positions, and store the offsets of terms.

- TermVector.NO: Don't store any term vector information.

Term vectors store myriad metadata about the terms for the field that has the term vector enabled. Information stored includes the following:

- Document ID

- Field name

- Actual text of the term

- Frequency

- Position

- offsets

BooleanQuery

BooleanQuery is a fundamental construct used in querying Lucene and getting relevant documents. Because of its generic behavior and the diversity and expressiveness of its clauses, BooleanQuery is one of the most used query types.

BooleanQuery allows specifying multiple clauses and their significance in the entire scoring/selection process.

The boolean model was discussed in Chapter 2 — this chapter talks about BooleanQuery implementation in Lucene.

You can assign three types of "levels" to a clause in a query:

- MUST: This clause must be matched by a document to be deemed a hit.

- SHOULD: These clauses are good to have and increase scores.

- MUST NOT: To be considered a hit, these clauses should not occur in the document.

The following method carries out a BooleanQuery:

```
private void booleanQueryExample(String firstQuery,
String secondQuery) throws IOException, ParseException {
  searcher = new Searcher(indexDir);
  long startTime = System.currentTimeMillis();
  Term firstTerm = new Term("foo", firstQuery);
  Query internalFirstQuery = new TermQuery(firstTerm);
  Term secondTerm = new Term("bar", secondQuery);
  Query internalSecondQuery = new PrefixQuery(secondTerm);

  BooleanQuery query = new BooleanQuery();
  query.add(firstInternalQuery, BooleanClause.Occur.MUST_NOT);
  query.add(secondInternalQuery, BooleanClause.Occur.MUST);
  TopDocs hits = searcher.search(query);
  long endTime = System.currentTimeMillis();
  for(ScoreDoc scoreDoc : hits.scoreDocs) {
    Document doc = searcher.getDocument(scoreDoc);
  }
  searcher. Close();
}
```

MultiTermQuery

MultiTermQuery is a query type that matches a subset of terms and returns corresponding results.

Multiterm queries are great when a query needs to filter by multiple terms. They are the equivalent of IN and NOT IN SQL constructs. Think of them as powerful tools for dynamic filtering. They prove especially useful when autogenerating queries through an application.

Multiterm queries require a FilteredTermsEnum to be passed in for defining the set of terms to be used for filtering. A FilteredTermsEnum is an iterator of terms, which is basically a subset.

Multiterm queries cannot be used directly (by invoking a constructor). Instead, they must be passed in a FilteredTermsEnum's concrete implementation, and then getTerms() needs to be invoked.

One popular version of MultiTermQuery is TermRangeQuery. TermRangeQuery allows specifying a range of terms to be used as the filter, both ends inclusive. Any term greater than or equal to a lower term and lesser than or equal to an upper term will match.

```
//Assume the index already exists
IndexReader reader = DirectoryReader.open(dir);
IndexSearcher searcher = newSearcher(reader);
TermRangeQuery query = new TermRangeQuery("content", new
Term("foo"),
  new Term("bar"), true, true);
searcher.search(query);
```

The preceding code defines a range of terms, from "foo" to "bar."

QueryCache

QueryCache proves useful when you want to enable heavy query performance. QueryCache defines an interface that allows caching queries at the junction when it is needed most: at the start of the query.

The QueryCache implementation used is LRUQueryCache. As the name implies, LRUQueryCache uses the Least Recently Used algorithm to evict keys when the cache is full.

As described in Chapter 2, each query creates a Weight instance (associated with the corresponding IndexSearcher). The default IndexSearcher implementation uses an instance of LRUQueryCache to cache the incoming query and create a cacheable Weight instance. When the scoring starts, the cacheable Weight instance checks whether the query is present in the cache. If it is present, the cached version is retrieved and returned. Otherwise, a cache load is done, and the corresponding instance is returned (see Figure 3-1).

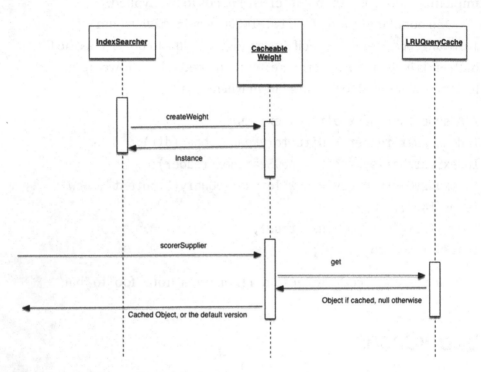

Figure 3-1. *QueryCache in action*

QueryCaches greatly speed up performance under high-load and repetitive queries. However, for a large number of distinct queries, QueryCaches can actually increase query latencies because of the additional query cache loading times. Also, if the query being cached is large, that becomes a significant overhead in the entire query's latency.

Weight represents the per-IndexSearcher statistics associated with a query. This is essential because it allows a query to be reused (as discussed with regard to QueryCache earlier in the chapter). Therefore, the same query can be used across multiple IndexSearchers, but each IndexSearcher will have its own Weight instance. Remember that Weight is correlated to IndexSearcher + Query, not just one of the two.

When a query is given to an IndexSearcher for execution, the IndexSearcher instance creates a Weight instance for the same. The lifetime of the Weight is limited to the query's execution lifetime within the IndexSearcher.

Weight is also responsible for participating in the scoring process. Weight creates the corresponding Scorer (described in the next section), and the Scorer is then invoked on various documents that the query is being evaluated against.

Note that the Weight is completely owned by the IndexSearcher. It is only maintaining statistics for a particular query, and the IndexSearcher is free to play with the Weight's data as much as it wants, with no side effects impacting other parts of the system.

Scorer as Part of the Search Process

Scorer is the core of the search process in Lucene. Scorer is responsible for identifying matches and scoring hits from the set of documents present.

Scorer is a special class. It is also an extension of a class known as DocIdSetIterator. DocIdSetIterator allows "iteration" over document IDs, thus allowing seeks over the index to get specific documents or to iterate over all documents. Note that the iterator can go forward only; it cannot go backward. This restriction simplifies the underlying codec supporting the iterator.

`DocIdSetIterator` provides three useful methods:

- `docID()`: Get the internal index document ID for this document. This method always returns monotonically increasing document IDs.

- `nextDoc()`: Iterate to the next document.

- `advance(location)`: Advance to the location specified.

This interface allows a `Scorer` to iterate over all documents and determine whether they are relevant to the query.

The `Scorer` works by implementing the `score()` method on top of the iterators. The `score()` method gets the current document ID, gets the current document, and returns a score for the same. `IndexReader` has statistics about the current document that can be fully utilized by the `Scorer` to determine a score. If term vectors are enabled for the field, the `Scorer` can get access to the term vector and perform even more elaborate operations.

How scoring is performed is discussed in Chapter 2. Here you'll see how it all fits together (see Figure 3-2).

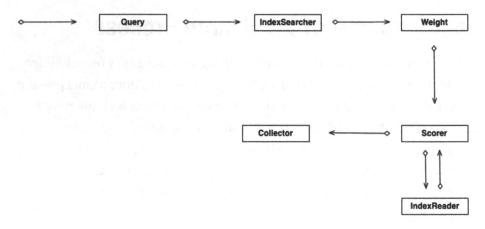

Figure 3-2. *A* Scorer *in a search*

The user issues a query with an instance of the Query class. The query is given to an IndexSearcher, which first rewrites the query recursively (invoking any modifications/simplifications if possible). Upon completion of the rewrite, an instance of the Weight class is created, which is specific to the Query + IndexSearcher combination. This Weight will contain all the query-specific statistics that apply to the execution of this query.

During the scoring, the Weight creates a Scorer, which iterates over all documents in the index, filters out the irrelevant documents, and applies the scoring algorithm on the candidate documents. The scoring algorithm can be anything that the user chooses to implement or use, but typically is a version of term frequency/inverse document frequency (TF/IDF) family.

The Scorer interacts with the IndexReader to get the relevant details from the underlying file directory. If a term vector is present, the Scorer can choose to use features from that as well to calculate the score for the document. The Scorer is expected to return a score per document it iterates on.

After scoring completes, the results are returned to the collector, which then chooses the next set of steps. If the top N hits are requested, the collector typically will maintain a priority queue to identify the top N hits and then return them back to the user.

CHAPTER 4

Spatial Indexing

Lucene provides a rich set of application programming interfaces (APIs) to index and query spatial fields, which allows for a variety of queries to be performed. Lucene allows either flat-plane or spherical models of spatial search.

Some key features of Lucene in that space are multidimensional points, latitude and longitudinal points, and box queries.

Lucene has a spatial module, which is the core engine responsible for spatial indexing and searching. The next section examines the API exposed by the module.

Spatial Module

The spatial module is based on Spatial4j, an Apache-licensed library that provides implementations for various shapes, such as points, rectangles, and circles, and additionally supports polygons with an extra dependency.

SpatialStrategy is the core interface used to interact with the spatial module, index spatial data, and perform spatial queries. SpatialStrategy defines the way to index and query based on shapes. From Lucene's javadocs, the points defined by a SpatialStrategy are as follows:

- Can it index more than one shape per field?

- What types of shapes can be indexed?

© Atri Sharma 2020
A. Sharma, *Practical Apache Lucene 8*, https://doi.org/10.1007/978-1-4842-6345-7_4

- What types of query shapes can be used?

- What types of query operations are supported? This might vary per shape.

Remember that if a different shape is attempted to be indexed than what is defined by the corresponding SpatialStrategy, an exception will be thrown.

Prefix trees form the foundation of spatial index data structures in Lucene. A prefix tree acts as a trie (a tree data structure where shapes are decomposed into strings, each string representing a rectangular spatial region). Figure 4-1 shows a prefix tree of the words "Car," "Cat," "Do," and "Don."

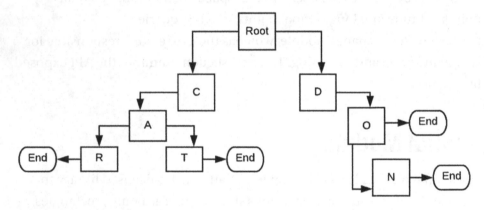

Figure 4-1. *A prefix tree*

Lucene defines an abstract class, SpatialPrefixTree, which represents abstract representations of a prefix tree. The class defines all the necessary methods, such as getting the number of levels, getting a cell at a level, and so on, that are required for working with prefix trees during searches.

As discussed in upcoming sections, Lucene consists of two concrete implementations of SpatialPrefixTree: QuadPrefixTree and GeoHashPrefixTree.

What Are Geohashes?

A geohash is a method of encoding an object of geographic information in the form of a short string of letters and digits.

Geohashes are hierarchal and offer variable precision (reducing the length of the representation by removing characters from the end of the string, and reducing the corresponding precision).

The value that geohashes bring is the simplicity by which two geographic information objects can be compared for similarity.

For two given objects represented in their geohash representations, a prefix match will give a value of how similar the two objects are. The higher the degree of the prefixes that match, the more the similarity between the two geographic objects.

`GeoHashPrefixTree` is based on the concept of geohashes, and it uses this technique to implement Lucene's `Prefix` tree class for similarity and matching.

Quad Trees

A quad tree is a spatial data structure where each node has exactly four children. A quad tree splits a spatial dimension into four each time a new level is added to the tree.

Quad trees are notable for two use properties:

- The higher-level nodes of quad trees help representation of the overall data in a less-granular level (i.e., the depth of detail stored in the top level is less than that stored in the leaf-level nodes).

- Quad trees are great for searching two-dimensional spaces. For example, given a two-dimensional space, to find a point closest to the given coordinates, a simple traversal of the quad tree will lead to the result.

Figure 4-2 shows a quad tree.

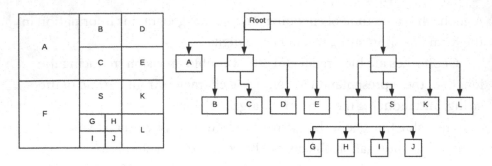

Figure 4-2. *A quad tree*

K-D Trees

A K-D tree is a space-partitioning tree that allows splitting a plane of space into a K dimensional space.

A K-D tree is a binary tree, with each node representing a K dimensional point. Put simply, given a collection of points, the range is split using an axis value. For example, if a node represents the X axis, and a split using the X axis is done, the left being all the points that have an X axis value less than the split value, the right tree having all values greater than the same.

K-D trees prove useful for a variety of query types, such as point and range queries. For this reason, they are an important member of Lucene's indexing capabilities. Figure 4-3 shows an example of a K-D tree.

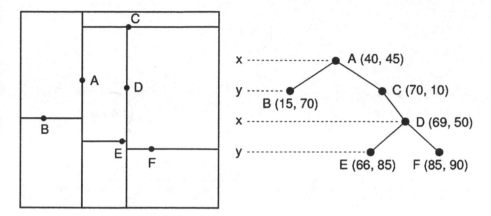

Figure 4-3. *A K-D tree*

Lucene's implementation uses a Block-KD (BKD) tree, which is an efficient version that is I/O friendly and restricts I/O usage.

BKD Trees

BKD trees are built in the same manner as K-D trees, recursing and partitioning the N dimensional space, and performing an equal split at each recursion. However, BKD trees stop recursing once there are fewer than 1024 points.

At that point, all points are written to one block on the disk.

When a point is indexed in the BKD tree, it is converted into its equivalent byte[] representation. Lucene then buffers the points being indexed and then writes them using a PointsFormat. All default Lucene codecs now support points being indexed.

As evident in Figure 4-4, a BKD tree is a K-D tree with a B tree incorporated into it. Nodes have compressed keys of their children and define key ranges with equivalent pointers into their children.

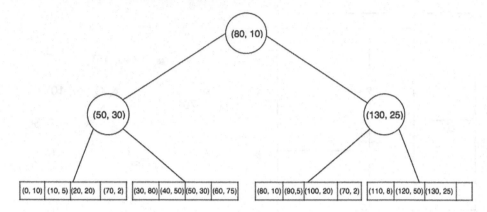

Figure 4-4. *A BKD tree*

Using Spatial Indexing

Let's now look at an example of how to use Lucene's spatial indexing capabilities to express spatial data and corresponding queries (the same example present in Lucene's repository).

We start by creating the index first:

```
final SpatialContext spatialCxt = SpatialContext.GEO;
final ShapeFactory shapeFactory = spatialCxt.
getShapreFactory();
spatialCxt.getShapeFactory();
// Define how the spatial tree will be constructed - we will
add prefixes to the tree using "Coordinates" as the key. The
maximum depth of the tree is 5
// being the tree to be used with level depth 5. "Coordinates"
is the field to be used as key.
```

```
final SpatialStrategy coordinatesStrategy = new
RecursivePrefixTreeStrategy(new GeohashPrefixTree(spatialCxt, 5),
"coordinates");

// Create an index
Final Directory directory = new RAMDirectory();
IndexWriterConfig iwConfig = new IndexWriterConfig();
IndexWriter indexWriter = new IndexWriter(directory, iwConfig);
```

Clearly, we are creating a geohash-based prefix tree on top of the standard IndexWriter class that we have seen before. This will now allow us to directly index points into the prefix tree using the created instance.

Now let's index some documents:

```
//Index some documents
var r = new Random();
for (int i = 0; i < 3000; i++) {
        double latitude = ThreadLocalRandom.current().
        nextDouble(50.4D, 51.4D);
        double longitude = ThreadLocalRandom.current().
        nextDouble(8.2D, 11.2D);

        Document doc = new Document();
        doc.add(new StoredField("id", r.nextInt())));

        var point = shapeFactory.pointXY(longitude, latitude);

        for (var field: coordinatesStrategy.
        createIndexableFields(point)) {
                doc.add(field);
        }
        doc.add(new StoredField(coordinatesStrategy.
        getFieldName(), latitude + ":" + longitude));
        indexWriter.addDocument(doc);
```

```
}
indexWriter.forceMerge(1);
indexWriter.close();
```

Note that the SpatialContext class being used is a class present in Spatial4j, a dependency of Lucene's spatial module. SpatialContext allows the creation of points from a variety of sources (in this context, from the latitude and the longitude). The point is then indexed into the data structure.

Now let's query the index:

```
//Query the index
final IndexReader indexReader = DirectoryReader.
open(directory);
IndexSearcher indexSearcher = new IndexSearcher(indexReader);

// Get the search range
double latitude = ThreadLocalRandom.current().nextDouble(50.4D,
51.4D)
double longitude = TheradLocalRandom.current().nextDouble(8.2D,
11.2D);

/// Approximate radius degree
final double NEARBY_RADIUS_DEGREE = DistanceUtils.
dist2Degrees(100, DistanceUtils.EARTH_MEAN_RADIUS_KM);

final var spatialArgs = new SpatialArgs(SpatialOperation.
IsWithin, shapeFactory.circle(longitude, latitude,
NEARBY_RADIUS_DEGREE));
final Query q = coordinatesStratefy.makeQuery(spatialArgs);
try {
        final TopDocs topDocs = indexSearcher.search
        (q, 1 // Number of docs);
```

```
        if (topDocs.totalHits == 0) {
                return;
        }

        // Get the doc
        var doc = indexSearcher.doc(topDocs.scoreDocs[0].doc);

        // Get the ID
        var id = doc.getField("id").numericValue();
} catch (IOException e) {
        e.printStackTrace();
}
```

Here we generate random latitude and longitude values. We then create a spatial "bounding box" of a circle with the relation that the point should be inside the circle. Hence, a point will be qualified as a hit only when it lies within the defined circle.

CHAPTER 5

Location-Aware Search Engines

Location-aware search engines are pretty crucial today, both as standalone search engines as well as components supporting business logic and operations (think of a food-delivery application). With the advent of location-enabled smart devices, this data is available more than ever, but that also signifies an information explosion in the amount of data that is available at any given point in time for such queries. Hence it is imperative that we build storage, indexing, and searching strategies that scale with the data while consistently delivering a reasonable degree of performance.

Note This is a theoretical chapter that builds on what we've covered previously. The concepts will help reinforce what you already know and give you a foundation for building a location-aware search engine.

Why Use a Search Engine for Geographic Searches?

Many geographic information system (GIS) tools that are available do the task of performing geographic searches. However, the advantage of leveraging a search engine for this use case is that you can combine

© Atri Sharma 2020
A. Sharma, *Practical Apache Lucene 8*, https://doi.org/10.1007/978-1-4842-6345-7_5

structured and unstructured data. This advantage implies that queries can be expressed that allow seeking across text and geographic data. A query can query on text data and create filters on geographic data and vice versa.

Another advantage of having search engines handle the functionality is the availability of things such as faceting, highlighting, and spell checking, which enable users to have greater control when expressing queries.

The next section first reviews some of the core query options exposed by Lucene that enable you to build such applications. The discussion then turns to geospatial searching basics, and then we work through a relevant project.

Knowledge of geospatial systems is not necessary, although it is good to understand latitude and longitude generalities. This chapter provides enough background context to help you make sense of the concepts covered.

Range Queries

Range queries and range filters allow you to restrict a given space of input. In a range query, the user specifies a bounding range. The bounding range acts as a bounding box for the documents in the index, and the query returns only the documents lying within the given range. This query model proves useful because it allows the application to filter down on geographic ranges and thus perform complex operations on only a subset of the dataset.

```
mod_date:[20020101 TO 20030101]
```

Internally, Lucene must enumerate all documents and match them against the given criteria to ensure that they match and choose only the ones that match the range (and discard others in accordance with the query). This process can be expensive, and so it is crucial to define the geographic data that you have so that these queries are not slowed down significantly.

Function Queries

Lucene also features function queries, which basically allow participation of the value of a field into the scoring mechanism instead of using just the default scoring mechanism. We use function queries to incorporate latitude and longitude data into our scoring mechanism later in this chapter.

```
q={!func}div(popularity,price)&fq={!frange l=1000}customer_
ratings
```

Geospatial Basics

When building a geospatial search engine, it is important to define how the data will be represented. A bad representation can lead to slow and inefficient queries, thus leading to an overall degraded end-user experience.

Geospatial data is typically available in various flavors. From high-level abstract models such as states and cities to granular forms such as latitude and longitude, geospatial data's form determines its use cases. Data such as countries and their general locations is good for things like world maps but not good for hyperlocal delivery apps (for which actual longitude and latitude are vital). Hence, there is no silver bullet.

Another consideration is the representation of the data in the search engine. Once we decide which data format we want to use, it is important to define how the data is stored in our indexes and how the query path works. In general, a bad representation can lead to an explosion in the size of the index, with a commensurate rise in the overall storage cost. In addition, Lucene queries are fan out, so the amount of data examined also increases, which can increase latency.

As you can understand already from this discussion, the use of a search engine often proves advantageous compared to using a pure GIS application. A search engine allows you to use multiple focal points to build a composite result. As mentioned earlier, a combination of data such as locations and semantic data can provide powerful insight to applications.

Representing Spatial Data

An obvious way to represent spatial data is to just store an identifier for the location. For example, consider indexing the name of a city as a token in the inverted index. Doing so allows for searching on the city name.

However, this method is restrictive because it allows just a single dimension of search to be performed. In this case, only search term queries on city names are served.

Therefore, we need to move to a deeper and richer data model that will allow finer queries to be served.

One thing to consider is the system used in our application to represent the said data. The spatial reference used to define the representation of the data being indexed is crucial. The most common spatial reference is the World Geodetic System, and we shall assume we are using a standard system across our engine.

The data that we will store for our search is latitudinal and longitudinal representation of the locations that we want to index and store. Latitude and longitude are generally expressed in degrees, minutes, and seconds from the prime meridian.

One catch when using latitudes and longitudes is the possibility of information explosion. This depends solely on how the overall geographic horizon is structured. What that means is that the granularity at which data is stored is of crucial importance. Too granular the data being stored, the larger the index size. Too macro level, the more degradation of search quality.

Figure 5-1 shows the size of the index with the increase in the granularity of the latitude and longitude pairs stored for the same geographic area. The X-axis represents the number of pairs stored, and the Y-axis represents the size in gigabytes (GB).

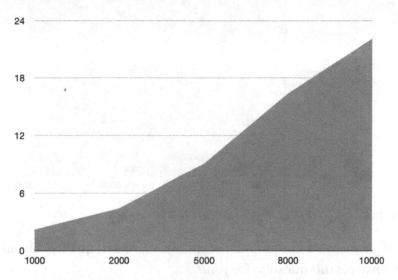

Figure 5-1. *Granularity vs. storage size*

Figure 5-2 shows the search precision vs. the index size. As evident, search precision eventually peaks out with increasing index size.

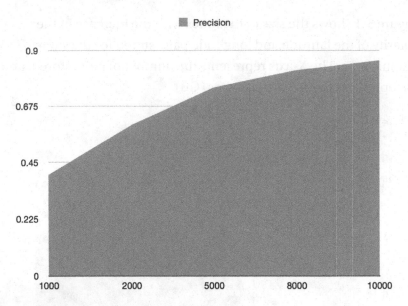

Figure 5-2. *Search precision vs. index size*

How do we solve this problem of storage vs. search quality? The next section answers this question for you.

Tiered Design for Storage

Instead of storing all latitudes and longitudes in the same index, we break down the overall geographic spectrum into areas. This trade-off between precision and storage is a way to reach equilibrium.

The division is done using Cartesian tiers. Each Cartesian tier focuses on a specific part of the geographic spectrum. For example, a tier may focus on one half of the city, and another tier may focus on a different part of the same city.

This design helps divide the data space into logical partitions, and helps in defining independent indexes for groups of partitions (thus reducing both the memory footprint of a query and the overall latency). However, because two different design layouts in the same engine can cause correctness issues, it is imperative to ensure that no confusion or ambiguity exists when inserting new records or reading the data.

Geohashes

Geohashes are a popular way to represent latitudes and longitudes. From Lucene's point of view, a latitude and longitude can be represented as two separate fields, but such a representation can result in query and indexing performance issues.

Geohashes provide an alternative way to represent this data. Representing the point on a Z order curve, a geohash is a hash for a given location. A Z order curve is a way of mapping multidimensional data to a single dimension without losing information.

Imagine the world divided into a grid with 32 cells. The first character in a geohash identifies the initial location as 1 of the 32 cells.

This cell will also contain 32 cells, and each of these will contain 32 cells (and so on ad infinitum). Adding characters to the geohash subdivides a cell, effectively zooming in to a more detailed area.

Figure 5-3 shows a geohash at three different levels.

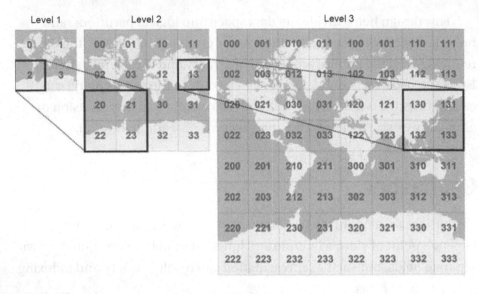

Figure 5-3. *Three levels of a geohash*

The use of a geohash allows indexing as a single field in Lucene and thus can save some performance cycles. However, the encoding and decoding cost their own CPU cycles (something to consider when performance planning).

Spatial Data with Text Search

A typical location search engine will typically have these requirements from the indexed data:

- *Distance calculation*: Given two points, calculate their distance.

- *Bounding box filter*: Given an area, find all documents that match in the area.

- *Sorting*: Sort all documents by their distance from an origin

- *Relevancy enhancement*: Use the distance as a boost in the ranking algorithm.

- *Query parsing*: Given an abstract query, convert it into an actual internal representation.

Distance Calculations

Suppose that we need to define a metric and a method to calculate the distance between two points. The easiest option is to treat the earth as a flat model and calculate the distance between two points using a Euclidean model. This model allows straight distance calculations with minimal complications. However, this model does not scale as distances grow and higher precision is needed.

The other option is to treat earth as a sphere and calculate distances using a spherical model. While more computationally expensive, this model provides better accuracy.

Bounding Box Filter

Bounding box filters are used to specify bounding filters for creating a candidate space of documents that match a geospatial filter. Consider a query that contains a textual filter and a geospatial filter. Since a geospatial index will contain a high number of points, it makes sense to first narrow down the set of documents to a small subset and then apply further filters on the subset to allow optimal performance of the query. This is where bounding box filters come in. Optimally, the first phase of a geospatial search should perform a high-level bounding box filter and then apply more sophisticated searching methods to the result of the first phase.

Typically, when latitudes and longitudes are stored in the system, you can define an area around a given latitude and longitude and thus define an area in which the documents involved are qualified and participate in the overall filtering at a higher level.

Note that you can ensure a higher degree of accuracy if the system use geohashes instead of latitudes and longitudes.

A Point on Distance Calculation

For search engines with geospatial searches, a key question is the distance algorithm used to serve and evaluate queries. Which algorithm you use depends on how accurate you want your searches to be. In some scenarios, being off by a mile is fine. In other scenarios, however, a few inches off may cause havoc.

In most cases, using Euclidean distance is good enough for all kinds of queries. However, for an earth-like model, the Haversine calculation algorithm works really well. For higher accuracy, Vincenty's model makes sense.

CHAPTER 6

Introducing Machine Learning with Apache Mahout

This chapter covers Apache Mahout and the synergy between Apache Mahout and Lucene.

Apache Mahout is a library of machine-learning algorithms designed to for scalability.

Origin of Apache Mahout

Mahout's origin derives from Apache Lucene. In 2008, Lucene had a few algorithms for doing some sort of clustering by default.

Lucene kept adding machine-learning algorithms on top of its existing capabilities, to a point where it did not make sense to keep the capability in Lucene but to instead make it an independent engine that could function on its own. This was the birth of the Apache Mahout project. Mahout started as a subproject of Apache Lucene and then became a top-level project.

© Atri Sharma 2020
A. Sharma, *Practical Apache Lucene 8*, https://doi.org/10.1007/978-1-4842-6345-7_6

Why Apache Mahout?

Apache Mahout is only one of the numerous ways in which machine-learning engines can be built. We are examining Apache Mahout here because it started as a subproject of Apache Lucene, and therefore Mahout has an inherent complementary architecture that supports machine learning on data present in Lucene.

Introduction to Machine Learning

Machine-learning uses range from game playing to fraud detection to stock market analysis.

Machine learning enables system builds such as Amazon's recommendation system, which attempts to divine user purchasing intentions, and such as Netflix recommendation system, which builds upon past viewing history and recommends related or complementary shows.

Machine learning leverages algorithms and mathematics to define the kinds of expected results. Categorization and filtering are two powerful use cases that apply machine learning.

Learning

Learning (in a machine-learning context) is the process of "learning" new information about the data and making decisions with a rising probability of being correct.

The two main types of learning are supervised and unsupervised learning:

- *Supervised learning* is when sample data is available for training the machine-learning model to anticipate and understand the expected output.

- *Unsupervised learning* works without any input data.
  Instead, it learns from results as it goes along. With
  this is mechanism, the algorithm starts from a very
  low correctness probability and then, using feedback,
  eventually works its way to more correct probability.

Clustering is a good way to perform first-level filtering and to eliminate
pieces that you do not want included in the final search results.

Collaborative Filtering

Collaboration is not a complex concept. Here is a simple example: If
you want to watch a movie, you ask your friends for recommendations.
Likewise, collaborative filtering takes a nearest-neighbor approach when
performing filtering. Figure 6-1 shows a collaborative-filtering model in
which users recommend items. As shown, Item 3 gets the highest rating
because both users recommend that item.

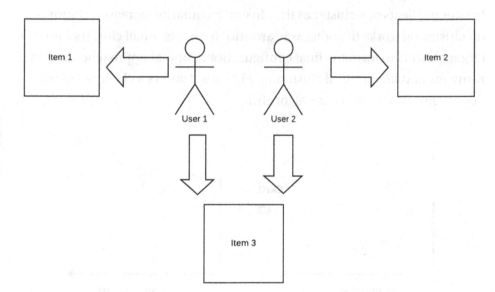

Figure 6-1. *Collaborative filtering*

Clustering

Clustering is the art of creating groups of similar objects.

Clustering involves segregating myriad objects into groups in which each group's objects are most similar to each other compared to their similarity to objects in other groups.

Clustering proves useful when you want to segregate objects into different buckets and then process them on a per-bucket basis.

Clustering and collaborative filtering are similar in the sense that they both calculate similarity between objects. However, clustering is involved only in the segregation, whereas CF goes a step further.

Given two vectors (value tuples), we can actually perform different analysis to determine the "closeness" of the two (such as Manhattan distance, cosine similarity, Euclidean distance, and so on).

The two most popular ways to cluster are top down and bottom up. Top-down clustering starts with a large cluster and iteratively breaks down the large cluster into smaller subclusters, with increasing similarity between objects of a cluster as the cluster granularity increases. Bottom-up clustering works the other way around. It merges small clusters into larger clusters to form the final configuration. Popular approaches include K-means and hierarchical clustering. Figure 6-2 shows a clustered set of documents using a K-means algorithm.

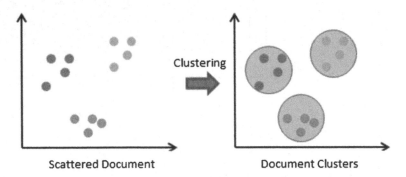

Figure 6-2. *Clustering*

Categorization

The goal of categorization (often also called classification) is to label unseen objects and thus group them together.

Categorization is putting the "unseen" in a known bucket as soon as it is viewed. This process can involve learning from previous candidates and seeing which kinds of properties the unseen object has, and then building a model using the known features of those properties to assign a category to the new object with a probability.

Features for classification can be anything that makes sense in the context of the object being classified. It can be parts of speech, tags, phrases, and so forth.

Converting from Lucene Components to Mahout Components

In the Mahout world, a feature vector is an object or a subset of a document. Explicitly, a feature vector is a tuple of attributes used for a document to represent a specific property. In a general case, it can be a set of weights.

Feature vectors form the basis of the integration between Lucene and Mahout. Most Mahout algorithms run off feature vectors.

Integrating Lucene with Mahout

The key difference between Lucene and Mahout is that Lucene requires features that enable a search and Mahout requires features relevant for machine learning.

There are two standard ways to integrate Lucene with Mahout, as discussed in the following two subsections.

lucene.vector

The `lucene.vector` utility enables the conversion of Lucene vectors to Mahout vectors. Note that the version of Lucene that creates the vectors should be the same as the Lucene vector used in Mahout.

The first step is to create term vectors before the conversion.

Here, we create a field with term vectors:

```
Field fld = new Field("text", "foo", Field.Store.NO, Field.
Index.ANALYZED, Field.TermVector.YES)
```

Convert the created Lucene index directly in Mahout with the following:

```
<MAHOUT HOME>/bin/mahout lucene.vector -dir <PATH TO INDEX>/
example/solr/data/index/ -output /tmp/ foo/part-out.vec -field
title-clustering - idField id -dictOut <Path>
```

Lucene2seq

The preceding section showed you how to convert Lucene term vectors into Mahout vectors for Mahout incorporation and processing. This section shows you how to convert Lucene stored fields into Mahout consumable objects (and thus available for Mahout processing). Run the following to see the options:

$ bin/mahout lucene2seq – help
```
Job-Specific Options:

--output (-o) output        The directory pathname for
                            output.

--dir (-d) dir              The Lucene directory
```

--idField (-i) idField containing the id	The field in the index
--fields (-f) fields index containing text	The stored field(s) in the
--query (-q) query Defaults to	(Optional) Lucene query. MatchAllDocsQuery
--maxHits (-n) maxHits Defaults to 2147483647	(Optional) Max hits.
--method (-xm) method sequential or mapreduce	The execution method to use: mapreduce. Default is
--help (-h)	Print out help
--tempDir tempDir directory	Intermediate output
--startPhase startPhase	First phase to run
--endPhase endPhase	Last phase to run

The tool fetches all documents and creates a set of key-value pairs, the key being the value of the ID of the field and value being a concatenated value of the stored fields associated with that key.

Lucene2seq converts into sequence files (which are Mahout components).

Java Version of Lucene2seq

Another way to use lucene2seq is to write a Java program. An equivalent Java class is LuceneStorageConfiguration:

```
LuceneStorageConfiguration luceneStorageConf = new Luc
eneStorageConfiguration(configuration, asList(index),
seqFilesOutputPath, "id", asList("title", "description"));

LuceneIndexToSequenceFiles lucene2Seq = new
LuceneIndexToSequenceFiles();

lucene2Seq.run(luceneStorageConf);
```

Putting It All Together

In this section, we use everything discussed in this chapter to write a clustering program for Mahout with data accumulated from Lucene indexes.

Note that this uses LuceneIndexToSequenceFiles to convert Lucene indexes to Mahout sequence files.

It then performs clustering based on standard Mahout techniques (with nothing Lucene specific in this part of the code):

```
import org.apache.hadoop.conf.Configuration; import org.apache.
hadoop.fs.FileSystem; import org.apache.hadoop.fs.Path;
import org.apache.hadoop.io.IntWritable; import org.apache.
hadoop.io.SequenceFile; import org.apache.hadoop.util.
ToolRunner; import org.apache.mahout.clustering.Cluster;
```

```
import org.apache.mahout.clustering.canopy.CanopyDriver;
import org.apache.mahout.clustering.classify.
WeightedPropertyVectorWritable;
import org.apache.mahout.clustering.kmeans.KMeansDriver;
import org.apache.mahout.common.distance.
TanimotoDistanceMeasure;
import org.apache.mahout.text.LuceneStorageConfiguration;
import org.apache.mahout.text.SequenceFilesFromLuceneStorage;
importorg.apache.mahout.vectorizer.
SparseVectorsFromSequenceFiles;

import com.google.common.collect.Lists;
import java.util.Arrays;
import java.util.List;

//Perform a simple K-means clustering to segregate documents
public class SimpleKMeansClustering {

  public static void main(String args[]) throws Exception {

    Configuration conf = new Configuration(); FileSystem fs =
    FileSystem.get(conf);

    //Use Lucene indexes as input data sources
    Path indexFilesPath = new Path("lucene/indexes/
    educations");

    //ML model data inputs—training data

    Path sequenceFilesPath = new Path("clustering/testdata/
    sequencefiles/");

    Path sparseVectorsPath = new Path("clustering/testdata/
    sparsevectors/");
```

```
//For TF IDF calculation
Path tfVectorsPath = new Path("clustering/testdata/
sparsevectors/tf-vectors");

Path inputClustersPath = new Path("clustering/testdata/
input-clusters");
Path finishedInputClustersPath = new Path("clustering/
testdata/input-clusters/clusters-0-final");

Path finalClustersPath = new Path("clustering/output");

//Create sequence files from a Lucene index
LuceneStorageConfiguration luceneStorageConf = new LuceneSt
orageConfiguration(conf, Arrays.asList(indexFilesPath),
sequenceFilesPath, "id", Arrays.asList("name", "description"));

SequenceFilesFromLuceneStorage sequenceFilefromLuceneStorage
= new SequenceFilesFromLuceneStorage();
sequenceFilefromLuceneStorage.run(luceneStorageConf);

//Generate Sparse vectors from sequence files
generateSparseVectors(true, true, true, 5, 4,
sequenceFilesPath, sparseVectorsPath);

//Generate input clusters for K-means (instead of having K
//randomly initiated)
TanimotoDistanceMeasure tanimoDistance = new Tanimoto
DistanceMeasure();

CanopyDriver.run(tfVectorsPath, inputClustersPath,
tanimoDistance, (float) 3.1, (float) 2.1, false, (float)
0.2, true);

//Generate K-means clusters
```

```
KMeansDriver.run(conf, tfVectorsPath, finishedInput
ClustersPath, finalClustersPath, 0.001, 10, true, 0, true);

//Read and print out the clusters in the console
//SequenceFile.Reader reader = new
SequenceFile.Reader(fs, new Path("clustering/output/" +
Cluster.CLUSTERED_POINTS_DIR + "/part-m-0"), conf);

IntWritable key = new IntWritable(); WeightedPropertyVector
Writable value = new WeightedPropertyVectorWritable();

while (reader.next(key, value)) {
  System.out.println(value.toString() + " belongs to cluster " +
  key.toString());
}

reader.close();
}

//Use Mahout to generate weights
public static void generateSparseVectors (boolean tfWeighting,
boolean sequential, boolean named, double maxDFSigma, int
numDocs, Path inputPath, Path outputPath) throws Exception {

List argList = Lists.newLinkedList();

argList.add("-i");
argList.add(inputPath.toString());
argList.add("-o");
argList.add(outputPath.toString());

if (sequential) {
  argList.add("-seq");
}

if (named) {
```

```
      argList.add("-nv");
    }

    if (maxDFSigma >= 0) {
      argList.add("--maxDFSigma");
      argList.add(String.valueOf(maxDFSigma));
    }

    if (tfWeighting) {
      argList.add("--weight");
      argList.add("tf");
    }

    String[] args = argList.toArray(new String[argList.size()]);

    ToolRunner.run(new SparseVectorsFromSequenceFiles(), args);
  }

}
```

CHAPTER 7

Improving Lucene's Performance

This chapter focuses on how to tune Lucene for optimal performance. You can use Lucene in multiple ways, but core performance ideally focuses on two aspects: indexing and querying (as discussed throughout this chapter).

This short chapter provides pointers for problem solving and is therefore light on theoretical concepts. The contents of this chapter build on what you've learned in earlier chapters. Here we just discuss best practices. The chapter does not really introduce anything new. (And because you have carefully read through the book to this point, you already understand the reasoning behind most of these practices.)

Increase Indexing Speed

Let's start with speed increases:

- Reduce the number of concurrently open writers. Open one writer and use it for the duration of the session.

- Too many concurrent writers can cause an excessive load and thus cause a general slowdown in the write performance. You should use a single writer throughout the cycle of existence of the search application.

© Atri Sharma 2020

A. Sharma, *Practical Apache Lucene 8*, https://doi.org/10.1007/978-1-4842-6345-7_7

Reuse Field Instances

To add new documents, create `Field` instances, assign them values, and then assign them to a document. Post the addition of the document to the index, reassign values to the fields, assign them to a new document, and add the new document.

The Curious Case of Large Commits

`IndexWriter` instances can create excess overhead when merging large files. Switching to `autoCommit=false` ensures optimal performance in such cases. However, such a switch also leads to open searchers not being able to see changes until the `IndexWriter` is closed. The ideal method is to chunk data in smaller blocks (batch your documents) and keep `autoCommit` to true.

Reuse Tokens in Analyzers

Analyzers create a new token for every term in the sequence.
    Reusing tokens is a sensible strategy to follow.

```
StoredFieldsWriter.MergeVisitor.tokenStream(Analyzer analyzer,
TokenStream reuse)
```

Tuning Flush Intervals

Lucene enables you to define flush intervals based on different criteria, such as the number of documents or the RAM usage. RAM usage flush intervals allow better utilization of RAM and result in less disk churn from frequent flushing when working with small/average document lengths. See the class `LiveIndexWriterConfig`.

Increase mergeFactor

Increasing mergeFactor by small deltas should increase the indexing speed.

Choosing the Correct Analyzers

Analyzers play an important role in indexing speed. Slow analyzers cause the overall indexing speed to decrease.

Use Multiple Threads with One IndexWriter

Using concurrency in IndexWriter can increase the indexing speed and utilize CPU core power better. However, there is a tipping point, so beware of overdoing it. The setting should be no more than the number of cores in the machine. See the setMaxThreadCount method of your MergeScheduler instance.

Index into Separate Indexes and Then Merge

If you have a very large amount of content to index, you can break your content into N "silos," index each silo on a separate machine, and then use writer.addIndexes to merge them all into one final index.

Improve Search Performance

This and the preceding section are not necessarily mutually exclusive and can depend on the kind of juice you are focusing on for your indexing. Remember that indexing and search are mostly happening on the same machine and that a resource overlap can happen.

Use the Latest Version of Lucene

If you are not using the latest version of Lucene, you risk missing out on upgrades and the latest of what Lucene has to offer.

Use IndexReader with the readOnly Attribute Equal to True

Using IndexReader with readOnly=true reduces thread contention to some extent and thus improves performance.

Use MMapDirectory/NIOFSDirectory

Both MMapDirectory and NIOFSDirectory give a substantially better I/O performance and thus improve overall performance. Note that NIOFSDirectory and MMapDirectory implementations face file-channel issues in Windows. It is best to use FSDirectory.open(), and Lucene will give the appropriate Directory implementation to the current environment.

Decrease mergeFactor

A reduced mergeFactor will lead to a fewer number of segments and thus reduce the fan out and hence improve query performance. However, this can be detrimental to performance of indexing and so needs to be done carefully.

Ignore First Query's Performance

The first query usually deals with cold caches, so disregard its performance. You need a larger dataset to be give you a holistic answer regarding performance characteristics.

Avoid Reopening IndexSearcher Instances

Reopening IndexSearcher instances is expensive. Don't do it unless absolutely necessary.

Share IndexSearcher Instances

Continuing the previous point, it is a good idea to share IndexSearcher instances to so that you have less contention.

Use Stored Fields and Term Vectors Sparingly

Stored fields and term vectors typically constitute a significant portion in the overall memory usage of the system. Indiscriminate usage of these can lead to a higher memory footprint.

Use Filters

Filters can reduce the overall disk seek that needs to be done by Lucene to fetch the required hits for a result set. Filters disable score computation and reduce the dataset being looked at. Wrap the query in ConstantScoreQuery or use filters.

Final Thoughts on Best Practices

While not a conclusive list, this chapter identified some ways to improve the overall performance of indexing and search in Lucene. Keep in mind that it is easy to optimize early and then see degraded performance. A better strategy is to first build your search application using vanilla configurations and measure performance. Only after you identify bottlenecks should you focus on improving performance.

CHAPTER 8

Your First Lucene Patch

This chapter covers some best practices for contributing to Apache Lucene. The walkthrough provides details about the Apache Software Foundation, the Apache way, and how to write your first patch and interact with the community.

Why Contribute to Open Source Projects?

Contributing to open source projects can be intimidating. Everyone is busy. Perhaps you have a million other things to do. Why would you want to contribute to open source and not do something else instead?

This is a tricky question, and everybody has different motivations for contributing to open source. Read on for some of the common motivations. Some of these might encourage you to contribute.

Improve Projects Based on Real-World Experience and Proven, Working Solutions

This is a no-brainer. We use a piece of open source software and realize that it can be improved based on our use case and actual experience with it. Active actual user feedback enables improvement of the product. You'll feel warm and fuzzy contributing code back to products you love.

© Atri Sharma 2020
A. Sharma, *Practical Apache Lucene 8*, https://doi.org/10.1007/978-1-4842-6345-7_8

Discover and Share Project Internals

Your contribution to an open source project may help a user learn more about the product/project and the internals of the system being using. Your contribution might even lead to a deeper usage pattern, where the use is based on an enhanced understanding system operation.

You might enable users to leverage the system in the best manner possible while also avoiding complex/costly pitfalls. Open source contributions are also a great opportunity for you (and other users) to enter the engineering space and peek under the hood. You can learn from this because most popular open source projects are engineered to perfection and have a high-quality bar for submissions.

Enhance Your Reputation, Boost Your Career

Contributing to an open source project can help establish/enhance your reputation and credibility as an engineer and developer. You have the change to showcase your capabilities, and because the Internet is written in ink and not pencil, your contributions are everlasting and ever-present. Your contribution can be referred to whenever needed.

Mitigate Future Risks

Unlike a closed source project, an open source project publishes its roadmap clearly and is also explicit about risks such as end of life, deprecations, and component removal. Being part of the open source community for a project you care about can help alleviate these risks while ensuring that you are able to plan for the future, know what is on the horizon, and note salient points of interest in upcoming releases.

Derive Personal Satisfaction

You might just have a desire to contribute to an open source project for the sake of contributing and building something that might potentially affect a lot of people. What else can you do to impact the world in such a massive way?

How to Contribute to Open Source Projects

Although there is no strict process to contribute to an open source project, the following steps generally work well when looking to contribute a feature:

1. Determine which part of your solution is worth contributing.

2. Study the contribution guidelines of the target project.

3. Obtain and build the project.

4. Extract the relevant code fragments.

5. Adapt the code and integrate the desired changes.

6. Provide the required level of automated test cases and documentation.

7. File an issue.

8. Submit the change.

Apache Software Foundation

From Wikipedia:

The Apache Software Foundation /əˈpætʃi/ (ASF) is an American nonprofit corporation (classified as a 501(c)(3) organization in the United States) to support Apache software projects, including the Apache HTTP Server. The ASF was formed from the Apache Group and incorporated on March 25, 1999.[2][3]

The Apache Software Foundation is a decentralized open source community of developers. The software they produce is distributed under the terms of the Apache License and is free and open-source software (FOSS). The Apache projects are characterized by a collaborative, consensus-based development process and an open and pragmatic software license. Each project is managed by a self-selected team of technical experts who are active contributors to the project. The ASF is a meritocracy, implying that membership of the foundation is granted only to volunteers who have actively contributed to Apache projects. The ASF is considered a second generation[4] open-source organization, in that commercial support is provided without the risk of platform lock-in.

Note that the foundation is based on the principles of decentralized, free software and focuses on meritocracy and a consensus-based software development approach. These represent the core principles on which the Apache Lucene/Solr community is based. Potential contributors need to be aware of these principles and respect all standards their standards. After all, a core idea of the Apache Software Foundation is "community over code."

Working with Git

To interact with the community and create patches, potential contributors must have a basic knowledge of Git. Git is the CVS that the Lucene/Solr community uses, and contributing is made easy by raising pull requests.

Basic Git Terminology

Blobs

Blob stands for Binary Large OBject. A blob is an generic way of storing and representing a file in Git. Any file changed in a Git-controlled repository is represented in a delta as a blob.

Trees

A tree is an object that represents a directory. It holds blobs and other subdirectories. A tree is a binary file that stores references to blobs and subtrees. (These references are also called the SHA-1 hash of the tree object.)

Commits

A commit holds the current state of the repository. Every commit is like a node in a linked list, with each commit having a pointer to its parent commit (and thus allowing a chain of hierarchy to be built). Every commit is named with the SHA-1 of its content. If a commit has multiple parent commits, that particular commit has been created by merging two branches.

Branches

Branches are used to create another line of development. By default, Git has a master branch, which is same as a trunk in Subversion. Usually a branch is created to work on a new feature. Once the feature is completed, it is merged back with the master branch, and we delete the branch. Every branch is referenced by HEAD, which points to the latest commit in the branch. Whenever you make a commit, HEAD is updated with the latest commit.

Tags

Tags are used to mark checkpoints in the repository. Think of tags as read-only branches that are snapshots of given branches. Typically tags are used to mark releases, but they can be used for other purposes as well.

Clones

Clones are used to create a copy of the entire repository. A clone is not just a mirror; it is a fully functional copy of the main code base. Generally these are used to keep local copies of the code.

Pull

A pull operation copies the changes from a remote repository instance to a local one. A pull synchronizes two repositories and allows changes from the main one to be synchronized into the fork.

Push

A push operation allows local changes to be pushed to the remote repository.

JIRA

JIRA is the issue tracker used by the Apache Lucene/Solr community. JIRA is simple to use and is the default community interaction mechanism.

The simplest way to interact with the community when an issue is found is to raise a JIRA. Do proper due diligence before raising a JIRA, and include the following in your JIRA: the issue, steps to reproduce, proposed fix (if any), and so on.

Writing a Patch

If you have identified what you want to change in Lucene/Solr and have a good idea about how to do so, it makes sense to write a patch. A patch is a change delta. Think of it as a "change" you want to make in the code base.

How you do this is by first forking the Lucene/Solr code base on Github. Post that, and then clone the repository by using git clone. Post that, and then create a branch by using git checkout -b <foobar>. Remember that the commit that you raise into the Lucene/Solr code base has to be marked with the JIRA number of the JIRA that you are working against. So, ensure that you have set up the JIRA number beforehand.

After making the changes locally in your repository, do a git diff to ensure that you have written the code the way you want and that no unintended changes occurred.

Do a git commit to create a commit and ensure that you have it pushed to your fork.

Tests

Here is an important reminder: Test every change and validate all functionality that your patch affects. You also need to confirm that all existing tests pass; there are no regressions.

It is a good idea to run ant test on the project to ensure that all tests pass. If a specific test is causing issues, use the following:

```
ant beast -Dtestcase=<Test Case> -Dtests.method=<Test Method>
-Dbeast.iters=<Number Of Iterations>
```

Writing Good Commit Messages

Although not fixed rules, these following guidelines apply when you write commit messages:

- Separate the subject from the body with a blank line.

- Limit the subject line to 50 characters.

- Capitalize the subject line.

- Do not end the subject line with a period.

- Use the imperative mood in the subject line.

- Wrap the body at 72 characters.

- Use the body to explain what and why vs. how.

Writing Documentation

You need to accompany any nontrivial changes with proper documentation (in code, configurations, and reference documents). Doing anything less will result in less-than-positive feedback from the community.

Raise a Pull Request

Now that you have completed a review-ready patch, you're ready to raise a pull request. Go to Github's UI and raise a pull request from your repository. Make sure that you track comments on it, actively iterate, respect feedback, and improve it. Hopefully, your changes will be incorporated.

Interacting with the Community

It is a good idea to drop an email to dev@lucene.apache.org stating your changes and asking for feedback. Generally, people will respond with constructive feedback. Remember that the most important goal is to improve the project; so although your work might be criticized, take it as constructive criticism.

Being a good community member is important, so you want to follow decorum and respect established norms and standards.

Index

© Atri Sharma 2020
A. Sharma, *Practical Apache Lucene 8*, https://doi.org/10.1007/978-1-4842-6345-7

Printed in the United States
By Bookmasters